PROPERTY OF
ST. CLEMENT'S
LIBRARY
ROSEDALE, MD.

MONSTER RIDDLES

Text copyright © 1993 by The Child's World, Inc.
All rights reserved. No part of this book may be
reproduced or utilized in any form or by any means
without written permission from the Publisher.
Printed in the United States of America.

Distributed to Schools and Libraries
in Canada by
SAUNDERS BOOK COMPANY
Box 308
Collingwood, Ontario, Canada 69Y3Z7 / (800) 461-9120

Library of Congress Cataloging-in-Publication Data
Woodworth, Viki.
Monster riddles / written and illustrated by Viki Woodworth.
p. cm.
Summary: A collection of riddles about monsters, including
"Who belongs to the Monster PTA? Mummies and deadies."
ISBN 0-89565-863-1
1. Riddles, Juvenile. 2. Monsters – Juvenile humor.
[1. Riddles. 2. Monsters – Wit and humor.] I. Title.
PN6371.5.W66 1993   91-46221
818'.5402–dc20   CIP / AC

MONSTER RIDDLES

Compiled and Illustrated by
Viki Woodworth

What do you call a huge rainstorm caused by a monster?
A monst-oon (monsoon).

What kind of Chinese food does a monster eat?
Mon-stirfries.

Why do monsters like to eat snowmen?
They melt in their mouths.

What kind of monster introduces acts at a variety show?
The Monster of Ceremonies.

How did the grandma monster knit a car?
With steel wool.

When you go to monster modeling school, what do you wish to become?
A cover ghoul.

Why was the monster not allowed to sing in the graveyard?
He couldn't carry a tomb.

What does Sherlock Monster solve?
Monsteries.

When doctors operate on a monster, what do they take out?
Ghoulstones.

How long are the monster's legs?
Long enough to reach the ground.

Who belongs to the Monster PTA?
Mummies and deadies.

Where do you find monster snails?
At the end of the monster's fingers.

Where does a zombie keep its hands?
In a handbag.

Was the zombie joking when he asked for a raise?
No, he was dead serious.

How did the zombie girl look for a boyfriend?
She went out to see what she could dig up.

How are a zombie's towels monogrammed?
"His" and "Hearse."

What did the zombie eat for breakfast?
Ghost and jelly.

Where did the zombie go for vacation?
The Sa-horror Desert.

Where does Dracula keep his money?
In a blood bank.

What kind of boat does Dracula like to ride in?
A blood vessel.

What kind of fruit does Dracula crave?
Necktarines.

Why is Dracula no fun to be around?
He's a pain in the neck.

Why did Dracula get braces on his teeth?
To improve his bite.

How did the policeman catch King Kong?
He wore a yellow slicker and made banana noises.

What did the banana do when it saw King Kong?
It split.

What is King Kong's favorite cookie?
Chocolate chimp.

Why did the army give King Kong a medal?
For superior gorilla warfare.

What do you get when you cross a big gorilla with an airplane?
King Kong-corde.

What's the hardest thing about teaching ballet to a gorilla?
Finding a tutu to fit.

What kind of flowers do witches grow?
Marighouls.

How does a witch flirt?
She bats her eyelashes.

What witch loves to play croquet?
The wicket witch.

What do little witches have for breakfast?
Hex Chex.

What witch lights the stars?
A lights witch.

What do witches bring to a party?
Potluck.

Why did the Cyclops teacher cancel his class?
He had only one pupil.

Why did the two Cyclops get into a fight?
They couldn't see eye-to-eye.

What did the creature have with its meal?
Dread and butter.

Why did the creature wear purple tennis shoes?
His red ones had holes in them.

What's another name for a monster movie?
A creature-feature.

Where does a French creature dine?
At a beastro.

What do little vampires learn in school?
The alpha-bat.

When do little vampires stay up all night?
When they're studying for a blood test.

Why did the vampire rush to the doctor?
Because of his awful coffin.

Why did the vampire sit in front of a fan with a shotgun?
So he could shoot the breeze.

Who carries the flowers at a vampire's wedding?
The flower ghoul.

How does a book about mummies begin?
With a dead-ication.

How do you know if a mummy likes Christmas?
If he's all wrapped up in it.

Where do werewolves stay on trips?
Only at Howl-iday Inns.

Who does a werewolf pick up on the highway?
Witch-hikers.

How does Dr. Frankenstein act in an emergency?
Ghoul, calm and collected.

Is Frankenstein's monster funny?
Yes, he's a stitch!

Why can't skeletons follow directions?
Words go in one ear and out the other.

How does the skeleton get into his house?
With a skeleton key.

What kind of china do skeletons use?
Bone china.

Why did the skeleton lose the race?
His heart wasn't in it.

How do we know skeletons aren't very brave?
They have no guts.

What famous skeleton fell apart?
Napoleon Bone-apart.

What does the creature from the Black Lagoon eat for lunch?
Fish and ships.

Why did the mother sea creature scold the little sea creature for chasing an octopus?
It was playing with its food.

What is green, slimy and gives sermons?
The preacher from the Black Lagoon.

What is green and slimy with gray hair and wrinkles?
The creature from the Black Lagoon when it's eighty years old.

What is green, slimy and begs to be forgiven?
The beseecher from the Black Lagoon.

What is green, slimy and has a horrible singing voice?
The screecher from the Black Lagoon.

When is a ghost blue?
When it holds its breath.

Why didn't the ghost stay for a visit?
It was just passing through.

What do you call a classroom of ghosts?
A lot of boo-boos.

Where do you find the best ghost fashions?
In a boo-tique.

What did the eye doctor give the near-sighted ghost.
Spooktacles.

What is a ghost's favorite breakfast?
Scream of Wheat.

What did the six-legged monster say to the shoe salesman?
I need a new pair of shoes, new pair of shoes, new pair of shoes.

If the monster breathes oxygen during the day, what does it breathe at night?
Nightrogen.

What does the monster love to drink?
Ghoul-ade.

Why did the monster take a ruler to bed?
To see how long it slept.

What happened when the monster swallowed a light bulb?
It hiccuped with delight.

What do you call a student monster who throws giant spitballs and tosses desks out the window?
Teacher's Pet.

What's the two-headed monster's favorite ball game?
A double-header.

Where do monsters study?
In ghoul school.

How did the monster divide the ocean?
With a sea-saw.

Little monster: Mother, I hate my teacher.
Mother monster: Then just eat your salad, dear.

What kind of monsters fly to the moon?
Monsternauts.